WE DANCE

A Teacher's Collection of Miracles and Memories

Hallie,

  You are a precious dancer. God Bless You!

  Love,
  Ann Carroll

TOGETHER
WE DANCE

God led you to me and me to you.
He has something special for us to do.
Let's pray that we learn what our mission is,
and, together we know all we have is his.

God gave me to you and you to me.
It's part of his plan for what he wants us to be
He wants us to work hard for whatever it is,
and claim all our successes to be also his.

God sent you to me and me to you.
He works in our lives as we need him to.
He loves us so much and shows us the way.
So listen and act and pray everyday.

Together we make things happen.
Together we learn and love.
Together we sing, together we dance,
As we journey to reach him in heaven above.

Together WE DANCE

A Teacher's Collection of Miracles and Memories

ANN CARROLL

PROVIDENCE HOUSE PUBLISHERS
Franklin, Tennessee

Printed in the United States of America

00   99   98   97   96   1   2   3   4   5

ISBN: 1-57736-010-9

Book design by Jeff Carroll, Robertson Design

PROVIDENCE HOUSE PUBLISHERS
238 Seaboard Lane • Franklin, Tennessee 37067
800-321-5692

CONTENTS

Together We Dance   ii
Preface   vii

Part One — Dance Children Dance   1
Heaven on Earth • Sharing in the Life of a Child • A Little Help • The Answer • A Best Friend • Unite Us • Pray and Things May Be Perfect • God's Call • M is for Memories • Thoughts on Teaching • Thy Will Be Done • Beth's Guardian Angel

Part Two — Miracles and Memories   17
The Last Word • Be Patient and Believe • A Good Neighbor • The Touch of Your Hand • Comfort Zone • My Word • Answered Prayer • Love with No Barriers • My Mental Journey • Send Me an Angel • Work It Out • Make Me Aware • Prayerful Patience • Just One of Thousands • An Angel in Disguise • OK — No Shoes • A Job Made in Heaven • Tickets To Go • Spiritual Friends • Perfect Timing • One Call • I Promise • Let Us Be Connected • A Need for Applause • Cheer Us to Heaven

Part Three—The Circle's Complete   **47**
For My Students • Because of You • For
All Teachers • For All Parents • For My
Children • Full Circle Dance

About the Author   **56**

PREFACE

As a young child, I was intrigued by angels. My mother would constantly remind me that my guardian angel was always with me—to light, to guard, to rule, and to guide. I was also reminded that angels come along, as people, to help us. Angels have been a part of my life for over fifty years. Thus, the new fascination with them has made me feel that the general public is experiencing a rather commercialized fad loosely based on thoughts that once seemed uniquely mine. It is my hope that readers will find the joy in angels that I have experienced and will continue to encounter the rest of my life. Some of my stories will show my awareness of and belief in my angels and how they assisted in my miracles.

I am very honored and humbled that I have been given a means to share with you the special stories that the Lord has allowed me to experience. In no way do I feel that I have been chosen, above anyone else, to participate in these small miracles. Each of us can be used, by the Lord, in so many ways if we just listen and act. It would have been very easy for me, as a shy person, to stay at home and consume myself with only my husband, my children, and my home. Because I have always wanted to do the right things in my life, I have had to consistently stretch out of my comfort zone. It has not been easy. Sometimes I have had to do things that have embarrassed me or made me feel foolish. There have been times when I have been led to do something that was not well received and I have wondered, "Lord, did I hear you right?" I am certainly not a *goody-two-shoes* who never makes mistakes when dealing with people—*I have failed him*. I pray, though, that I can learn from each mistake.

Being a private person, I know that in writing this book I have opened myself up for criticism. I also know that I was led to do this—the way that this book became a reality is a miracle in itself. The remembrances presented here came to me so freely; they were read by people who encouraged me and, eventually by my publisher, the father of one of my students. Once again, I have stretched beyond my comfort zone! I invite you to come along with me.

PART ONE

DANCE CHILDREN DANCE

HEAVEN ON EARTH

God sent you to me for a reason.
   He knew you would —
      fill my heart to the brim with your love,
      touch my soul like he from above,
      hug me like a hand in a glove,
   But he sent you to me for a reason.

God sent you to me for a reason.
   He knew you would —
      lean on me when your heart's broken in two,
      share with me the things that you do,
      cry with me when you're feeling blue,
   So he sent me to you for a reason.

God sent you to me for a reason.
   He knew you would —
      learn to dance with your body and soul,
      make our weeks completely whole,
      keep us warm and never cold,
   So he put us together for a reason.
      He sent you to me to guide you.
      He sent you to me to serve you.
      He sent you to me to love you,
   And see a bit of heaven on earth.

SHARING IN THE LIFE OF A CHILD

After my husband earned his doctorate and was hired at a university in Nashville, we headed for Franklin, Tennessee, with all intentions of me being a full-time wife and mother. I had been teaching dance in a college for four years and privately for six years. About two weeks after we were settled and because I loved teaching, I decided to take just a *few* students to satisfy this need.

The only advertising I did was in the telephone Yellow Pages. There is something deep within me that makes it very uncomfortable to advertise for children. I feel a parent should search out, methodically, the proper match between the child and the dance school that will, hopefully, be a "home"—a place where she or he will grow physically, mentally, and spiritually.

The Lord had a plan for me, because when I turned around twenty-six years later, he had given me a *very large* business. I remember, about five years ago, when I stopped for a minute and realized that *all* of the bookkeeping and files were for a small business. What a scary thought to see that I was about twenty years behind! I was still trying to take care of each person just like I had at the beginning.

Lord, you have given me the desire to take care of each of my students and parents individually. Please give me the knowledge and the strength. Thank you, Lord, for giving me such a gift of sharing in the life of a child!

A LITTLE HELP

In a hurry to get my pointe class started, I saw Whitney trying to get her shoes on, but her pointe shoe only had one ribbon. I asked her where her other one was (so we could repair it) and she explained to me that she had given it to Molly to put her hair up. Since dance classes teach discipline, the students are all required to have their hair up, be dressed in a leotard, and have all shoes in working order. Whitney risked not having her shoes in order for Molly, who was very shy, to have her hair up.

This was very touching to me, so I praised Whitney for her act of kindness and told her I would find her another ribbon. In my rush, I had not said a prayer for help but ran to look in the costume room closets, shelves, and drawers where a ribbon could be found.

I became frustrated about not finding one, sat down at the desk in my office, and said, "Lord, Whitney deserves a ribbon for her pointe shoe. Please help me." When I opened my eyes and looked to the left, there, on a shelf where I had looked before, was a ribbon the exact width and length of a toe-shoe ribbon. I took the ribbon to Whitney and shared that I could not find a ribbon, but, the *Lord* did!

THE ANSWER

Jenny, a former teenaged student at my dance school, left a message on my answering machine and wished for me to return her call. My husband and I had been on a week-long vacation and she had called sometime during that week. Many messages were left during that period, but I had a strong feeling that I should return Jenny's call immediately. Because I was exhausted, I put the call off until around 10:30 that night.

Even though my husband felt this was much too late to be calling anyone, I picked up the telephone and dialed her number. Jenny answered the phone and obviously had been crying. She thanked me for returning her call and said that she had just been praying to talk to me about a difficult decision which she *had* to make by the *next morning*. Together, we determined what we believed to be the best decision for her.

A couple of weeks passed and Jenny called me to say thanks. She said that she had written a paper in school that day about her *first* spiritual encounter—one where she prayed in desperation and received an answer immediately. Lord, your timing is so perfect if we just listen!

A BEST FRIEND

As a dance instructor in a large dance school, I am given "opportunities" that are unrelated to dance but very important in the life of a child. Emily, a third grader, was giving her father a little resistance about coming to dance class. Her father shared that with me, and we decided that since she was new to the area, she might need help in finding a friend. After discussing this with Emily, who seemed excited about the idea, I explained to her that we needed to get the "just right" friend and that we could not do that alone—we needed help from the Lord. I told her to continue her dance class and I would go to my office and say a prayer for that special friend.

In my own mind, I had already chosen Katie, who was *also* new and *also* the same size as Emily (both the shortest girls in the class). But I had to make sure. When I am in a hurry and need an answer immediately, the Lord and I work out ways for a quick solution.

After praying I said, "Lord, the first person I think of, when I take that one step into my classroom, will have to be the friend you want for Emily." I still felt like I knew that it would be Katie. That was so logical to me! When I took that step, *Tori* popped into my head. I immediately thought, Lord, that couldn't be right because Tori was the *tallest* in the class—about two feet taller than Emily!

Wanting to be obedient, I got the two girls together and they seemed happy. I felt that *any* friend is better than no friend—still not completely agreeing with the choice the Lord had made.

The next week Emily's father came to the dance studio and thanked me for helping out. He said that it had really made a difference. In my mind I still kept thinking that any friend is better than no friend.

But then, later during the week, Tori's mother came to see me to thank me for what I had done for Tori. I asked her what had I done? She explained that Tori was having a difficult time in school and church because she had not felt needed. They had been praying about it, and I had made her feel needed.

After a moment of overwhelming thankfulness that I had been obedient and that our Lord is there for our small "opportunities" as well as the big ones, I explained to Tori's mom that I could not take the credit for the friendship — that I had originally (in my mind) chosen Katie but that the Lord had chosen Tori.

She asked me to share that with Tori. When I did, all Tori could say was, "You mean the *Lord* chose *me*?" Tears of joy were streaming down her face.

UNITE US

One of my students had been going through some trying teenage years. I was really one of the few people that she respected, so she would come to me "just to talk." I telephoned her one day to see how she was doing. She began talking so negatively about her parents. My usual approach was to listen and then she would somehow talk herself out of these feelings. This particular day she did not, so I began trying to make her understand that her parents were good people and they did what they had to do because they loved her. She started cursing at me and hung up the phone.

Evidently this child had serious problems but I certainly was not going to let that incident detract me from trying to help her. Dance was the one thing that she was extremely good at and that gave her confidence as a person.

Her mother phoned me a few days later and wanted me to talk to her so she would not quit dance. The mother told me her daughter was at a beauty parlor and asked if I could go there and speak with her. I explained, to the mother, that I wanted to do the *right* thing so I would pray about it. I needed some sort of answer between my home and the six or so miles to the beauty parlor. Was it best for her to come to me or for me to go to her?

On the way, I passed a church with a sign that always has messages that seem to be strictly for me. Usually, it took me two or three times to pass this sign before I could get the entire message. This particular time, however, I was the only car at the stoplight in front of this church. The message was directly to my left and I could take it all in. It read, "Do things that *unite* you, not *separate* you." The student came back to her dance classes and to me.

PRAY AND THINGS MAY BE PERFECT

Dr. Laurence Harvin, at Middle Tennessee State University, asked my students to dance at the Christmas concert with their symphony orchestra. He wanted us to do two dances and really wanted two singers but was afraid the concert would be too long. I told him that I would talk to Michael Pickern and Steve Flanigan, two wonderful singers, and if it was supposed to be, something would work out. Dr. Harvin agreed.

Dr. Harvin had already chosen the music for our two dances. I prayed that the best situation would happen for the concert. When I talked to Michael, he said that he had always wanted to sing "Santa Claus Is Coming to Town" and Steve said that he would really like to sing "O Holy Night." It miraculously happened that these were the exact songs that Dr. Harvin had chosen for us to dance to, so he got his dancers *and* singers together.

Lord, the way you work out details is so perfectly choreographed.

GOD'S CALL

The Lord never ceases to amaze me. How he works out details just like a puzzle fits together is awesome. As a dance school owner in Franklin, Tennessee, I was looking for an additional teacher to fill a staff vacancy. For this Christian-based school, which the Lord helped me build, the new teacher needed to be a special person.

In most résumés, the faith of the applicant is not mentioned. Only their dance, theatre, TV, movie, and teaching experiences are included, so this was going to be a real challenge for the Lord and me. After praying for guidance, I laid all the résumés in a line to read and study. This person must love to teach, love and be sensitive to children, love to learn, love challenges, and love the Lord. All of these résumés had been sent to me over a period of time, so I did not even know if any of the applicants were still available. When I had finished studying and learned that each of them possessed the technical, performance, and teaching background needed, I realized that "we" had to get into minor details — the wording of the applications and the feelings of each applicant.

Consistently asking the Lord for help, I kept coming back to a letter written by Kerry. Like most of the others, she had danced in television specials, appeared in movies in California, and taught for several years. The only thing I could find different was that in one sentence she had used the word *blessed*. That word kept hitting me like a brick. The Lord knows he sometimes has to use force to get my attention.

Kerry had included an out-of-state phone number, so I called her. She was *still* in search of a job. The puzzle was beginning to take shape. I described the responsibilities of the job and then told her that there was something about our school that she would either love or hate—it is a Christian-based school. I explained that we did not preach in class, but we never hesitated to give God the glory. Her immediate reply was, "Thank the Lord!"

It seems that Kerry had been praying for a job in the Franklin area, had heard about my school, and had wanted to be involved in a school like ours. She shared that she had almost given up hope because her letter had been written months before. At the time that I received her packet, I never expected to need another teacher.

We talked for a couple of hours and I told her that I would get back to her after my husband and I returned from a two-week vacation in Europe. This would give her the time to think and pray about the job. I wanted so much for it to be the best for both of us—the school and Kerry. When I called her back she accepted the teaching job and we were both excited about working together.

Then, some details had to be worked out, such as a place for Kerry's family to live. Since Kerry and her husband David lived in another state, arrangements had to be made by phone. Their needs included a place to rent with some land (not an apartment) that they could afford. David was in the midst of writing, producing, directing, and filming a movie and would not be able to move to Franklin until six weeks after Kerry arrived.

We all began to pray that the Lord would work all of this out quickly because Kerry had to begin teaching in mid-August. That gave "him" only three weeks and rentals in Franklin were scarce. We wondered if this might be asking too much, but we were to soon find out that it was not. Paige, a friend of Kerry's from high school, was in a beauty parlor in Franklin, and a woman came in and asked if anyone knew of a person who wanted to rent an apartment. Paige said she did and went to the location to check it out. It was an apartment in an older home, on many acres of land, with a lake, in the price range they wanted, and (a bonus) only two miles from the dance studio! Can you believe how wonderful the Lord is?

The only obstacle was that the owner was on vacation for two weeks and there was the possibility of it renting before she returned. Because the timing was important, Paige got the telephone number where the owner was vacationing and relayed it to Kerry. The next part of the story could only be the Lord working! The owner was vacationing only two miles from where Kerry and David were living in Cape Cod! They met and worked out the details of the rental halfway across the United States from Franklin, Tennessee. God's puzzle was complete!

After Kerry had been teaching a few weeks, she showed me a note on which she had written details of the job from our phone conversations. She shared with me that she had been concerned that, after the first call, I might not call back because the two weeks had passed for our European trip. David comforted her by praying and saying, "When God is ready, Ann will call."

Almost immediately, their phone rang. David picked it up, and, realizing it was me and that their prayer had been answered, gave the phone to Kerry and wrote on top of her note, "It's God's call."

M IS FOR MEMORIES

I treasure the memories of all my students who have graduated, and I love to hear from them. It had been about two years since I had heard from Julie C. She had married, and I did not remember her husband's last name. For one week, I could not get her out of my mind. I even looked through the phone book to see if I could jog my memory by looking at some of the names. My feeling was very strong that his name started with an M. Morris, maybe! I called four or five of the numbers hoping that I could hear Julie answer the phone. No luck!

The teachers and I were choreographing at the studio before classes one afternoon when I saw someone walk into the room. As she got closer I finally recognized her. It was Julie! She told me that she had experienced the same strong feelings to get in touch with me all week. She finally obeyed those feelings. Her last name was now Marsh.

Lord, thank you for seeing to it that people get together, especially those who have shared so many wonderful memories. Friendships are treasures to behold.

THOUGHTS ON TEACHING

I love teaching children of all ages. Each age has its special opportunities, but my heart goes out to teenagers, especially seventh and eighth graders. They will tell you immediately that Mrs. Ann truly loves them. It is such a complex age—they are either laughing or crying. They are sick often, they injure their bodies easily, and they tire quickly. These are not invented problems. They truly feel these things. Most of the time, these situations are caused by emotional upsets which result in sickness and injury to their bodies. Girls, and sometimes boys, at this age, hurt others' feelings to make themselves feel better. Eventually, and thankfully, in higher grades they realize that this does not work. In the meantime, I try to listen to their problems, provide them with relationship classes each year, put braces on their wrists, knees, and ankles, and understand when they sometimes do not give their all.

This is also the age where decisions can "make or break" them. Because I believe that a bad apple spoils the rest, I have taken a tough stand in that, if they make and act on a bad decision, I *will* find out and ask them to leave. Most of my students have chosen not to make those bad decisions, for whatever reasons, and go on to graduate from the dance school. They are told weekly that each year after the eighth grade gets better and better. They all rest assured that life goes up hill from there.

I do not hesitate to tell the students that I love life more today than yesterday and that I would never want to go back to any age unless I could take all my opportunities and experiences with me.

THY WILL BE DONE

After thirty-five years of teaching and owning a large Christian-based dance school, I have learned that the Lord sometimes speaks to me through the parents and the students. Occasionally, I would tell them about some of the stories that I had recognized as *miracles* and not *coincidences*. I wrote all of these stories in a journal.

Over the years, many people had been telling me that I needed to share them with others in a book. The idea seemed like another job, and I certainly didn't need that.

One night I was reading through my journal and realized that I had over fifty miracles with the Lord always the *technical director* and I in a minor role. I prayed that the Lord would show me if I was only supposed to enjoy them myself or share them with others. I wanted to do his will, but I needed a sign.

On Christmas morning, we were all opening our presents in our one-at-a-time choreographed manner. My youngest son Tim gave me his present a little reluctantly saying, "Mom, I don't know why I bought this for you, it's very much unlike anything I would give, but I couldn't leave the store without it." As I opened it, my first statement was, "Oh, no!" Tim said, "Mom, don't you like it?" I hugged him for the present and explained that the Lord had used him to give me an affirmation to my prayer. It was a cherry lap desk for writing! When I sat down to write the stories, they flowed out with no effort. There was no feeling of "another job."

Lord, when we truly want to do your will, you are always there to help us through.

BETH'S GUARDIAN ANGEL

Beth, a dance student of mine, lost her brother in an automobile accident while he was at college. Of course, it was devastating to her. Wishing I could somehow relieve her pain, and knowing it would take a long time, I vowed to her that I would pray for her and her family every day for a year. When I saw Beth at the funeral home and sometime later at her dance lesson, I told her that her *guardian angel* was always by her side to comfort her. In her tears, she once said, "I wish I could see the angel." Well, my prayers then became, "Lord, please show your light and comfort to Beth."

Andrea, also a student, came into my office sometime after the funeral and told me that at the funeral home she observed a white light around Beth's head. She thought it had been an *aura* and asked me what I thought. "I'd rather think it was a *guardian angel*," I said, as we both went back to our dance classes to concentrate on perfecting our art.

A few days earlier, Susan, a parent of three of my dance students, had taken photos of four of our demonstrators to include in *The Footnotes*, a monthly newsletter for the dance school. A week later, she brought the photographs in for identification and to choose one of each girl.

When I saw the pictures of Beth, I knew my prayers had been answered! Susan explained that she had taken all the photographs against the same wall with the same camera and the same film, and had taken one photo of each girl before deciding to take another photo of each. *Both* of Beth's pictures had a white circle around her head! I asked if I could give one of the pictures to Beth. When Susan agreed, I put the photo in a frame with an angel on the side. Across the top, the inscription read, *My Guardian Angel*.

PART TWO

MIRACLES AND MEMORIES

THE LAST WORD

On March 4, as I was praying for Betty, a dear friend in the hospital in a coma from the last stages of cancer, I felt strongly led to go to the hospital and tell her daughters to release their mother from her pain and suffering. She was never able to talk to her daughters about dying—they would only talk about her getting better—which made her even more concerned about her death. When they had taken her to the hospital a week before, the doctors felt that, from all indications, she would die during that first night. Betty had other plans—she was waiting for something.

Betty had many friends because of her bubbly personality and witty disposition. The special trait I loved was her ability to always have the last word which always made us laugh! Knowing that many friends had constantly been at the hospital and that I am shy and would not be able to talk to the girls alone, I argued with the Lord saying, "Why me?" Finally, I bargained with him saying that I would tell them if they were alone, feeling that I was safe from the task I was asked to do because I had never seen them alone.

When I got to the hospital, the girls *were* alone! They immediately sensed that I had something to say, so I sat them down and explained that I had been led there to urge them to let their mom go by telling her that they would miss her so much, but they wanted her to do something for herself now and go on to her heavenly peace. Betty was always concerned about others.

We agreed that this was the reason Betty was still living against all odds. After they went into her room and talked with her in her comatose state, the girls explained that a peace had come over them and that they felt very good about what they had done.

It was very difficult for the girls to see their mother linger this way so I offered to sit with her, knowing that Betty did not like to be left alone during the last months of her cancer. Within fifteen minutes she peacefully took her last breath!

On the way home, I was thinking of Betty and remembering all of her wonderful qualities, especially the one I loved the most—always having the last word. Suddenly, I realized that she had died on March 4, and thus, her last word to us was to *march forth* with our lives!

BE PATIENT AND BELIEVE

Before I was pregnant with my third child and right after I had delivered my second son, I began praying for a baby girl. Julie Ann was born four years later!

I have always thought red hair was so beautiful and special. Since my husband's father had red hair, I knew the genes were possible and after Julie's birth, I began praying for a red-haired baby. We really were not sure we should have a fourth child, but I started covering the wish just in case. Three years later, Timothy was born with the *blackest* hair I had ever seen and ten times more hair than any of the others. I even made the nurses double check to make sure he was ours! After they cleaned him up and brought him back to me, they all complimented his beautiful black hair. They were very amazed that he had *one bright red hair* sticking straight up. Recognizing this as a sign, I explained, "That red hair is an answer to three years of prayer for a red-headed child. The Lord is telling me that he's not giving it to me *now* but to be patient." The nurses and I knew that I would have no more children because of an RH-blood factor that my husband and I have.

I could not have any more children, so I thought the promise would be fulfilled in a red-headed grandchild. I have talked about my "red-headed grandchild" since my children were small. My second son Jeff *and* my daughter Julie *both* married red heads and Julie recently gave birth to a beautiful red-headed daughter—twenty-three years after the sign the Lord gave to me.

A GOOD NEIGHBOR

My husband and I bought a home that we both loved. He also loved the fact that on one side of our house there was vacant "commons" area, and, on the other side, there was a vacant lot owned by our neighbor. No one would build on either side of us.

I, on the other hand, wanted to have a neighbor close by. For five years it was fine, but after that time, I told my husband I was going to pray for the lot to sell. His reply to me was, "They will never sell that lot, and you're just setting yourself up to be hurt." I continued to pray. About a month later there was a "for sale" sign on the lot! After thanking the Lord for my special answer to prayer, and after dealing with my husband's amazement over the "for sale" sign, I then told him that I was going to pray for a *good* neighbor. His reaction again was, "You're setting yourself up to be hurt." Doesn't he ever learn?

A few months later I was coming up the stairs from work and my husband was on the phone. He put the phone down and just stood there for a minute, not saying a word. "Is something wrong?" I asked. He said, "You never cease to amaze me. That was a call from your neighbor who is building next door." It was Don and Gwen, who had been neighbors of ours twenty years before. We had carpooled our boys to school and were in a prayer group together. The Lord truly sent me my *good* neighbor!

THE TOUCH OF YOUR HAND

Many wonderful memories come to my mind when I remember my dear mother. Some are exclusively mine — like the feel of her hand on my forehead, affectionately brushing my bangs out of my face as she talked to me.

In her later years, she had Alzheimer's. I watched her transform from a loving, caring person able to take care of herself to a person living in a nursing home unable to recognize anyone. However, she always had an angelic smile on her face.

We lived in Franklin, Tennessee, and she lived in Natchez, Mississippi. At first, I would call her almost every night to talk to her. Eventually, she would not talk so I wrote her notes each day for the nurses to read to her. Soon, I lost all contact with her until I could get to Natchez. I would always leave there feeling ill because she never knew I was there.

The last time I went to see her, I prayed that somehow she would recognize me, even if it was only for a split second. I found her in a child-sized wheelchair. I ran in and knelt by her, so much wanting her to hug me. She turned to look at me as I talked to her. In the middle of a sentence, she lifted her hand and brushed my bangs off my forehead, just as she had done when I was a child. For a moment I *knew* that she recognized me! Thank you, Lord, for that gift. That was the last time she touched me before she died.

COMFORT ZONE

The Holy Spirit urged me to say something to each of my students at the end of our recital. Not me! I argued, "Remember, I am the one who could never speak in front of a class. I avoided all classes in college if I had to stand and talk, and I had to be pushed out on the stage to accept flowers from the students at the end of the recitals!" I wanted to stay in my *comfort zone*, so I wrote what I wanted to say and asked each of my teachers, one by one, if they would consider reading my message to the students at the end of the recital. Each of the teachers graciously told me that they *would* do it, if I insisted, but they felt that *I* should do it.

I tried to forget the whole idea, but when the Holy Spirit wants something done, there is *no way* to ignore the matter. After thinking about it, I decided to read my message from *backstage* to the students *onstage*. This would work!

A few days later, I found a tape on my desk. Since my teachers and I are always listening to new music to choreograph, I put the tape in the player. One of those songs had almost exactly the very same words I had written to *say* to the students! My teachers shared with me that they felt this was *not* a coincidence, and that I needed to *sing* that song to the students! *I am no singer!* Trying to always be obedient, I began rehearsing the song. I only practiced where *no one* else could possibly *hear* me or know what I *might* be thinking of doing—especially my family. Well, I *did* sing, to the surprise of everyone, to five hundred children; firmly believing that any mother can sing a love song to a child.

It now has become a recital tradition that the students will not let me discontinue; although it has not become any easier! Well, so much for my *comfort zone*.

MY WORD

Marriage encounter weekends are to strengthen a loving marriage rather than for marriages in trouble. Knowing this, my husband and I set out to experience this weekend. There was plenty of work involved in the weekend and we had worked our way down to the last hour. Each couple was told to look into their spouse's eyes and say one word that described their most endearing quality.

We were the last couple and I had heard words spoken such as wonderful, beautiful, spiritual, caring, loving—you know, all those romantic words that women *live* to hear. I could not wait until it was our turn so I could hear the word from my husband that would just put the icing on this weekend. Whenever he would give me an unsolicited compliment of *any* sort, I would hang on to it and remember when, where, why, and how he had said it. So, I was sure this would be my next treasure to save.

It was *finally* our turn and our eyes met, my heart racing with excitement as he said, "persistent!" I was crushed! What a harsh word for such a wonderful, meaningful occasion! He later tried to explain to me that he thought it a compliment and it was not meant to hurt me. He felt that it was a much deeper word than all the "fluffy" ones that he had been hearing.

After the weekend, it was forgotten except when I felt the need to bring up "dirty laundry." Each time, he would insist that he meant it as a compliment.

About ten years later, I was reading one of my Christian magazines and suddenly I saw, on the lower right-hand corner of a page, and not much bigger than a postage stamp, *that word*! It read:

Nothing in the world can take the place of persistence. Talent will not; nothing is more common than unsuccessful men with talent. Genius will not; unrewarded genius is almost a proverb. Education will not; the world is full of educated derelicts. Persistence and determination alone are omnipotent. The slogan "press on" has solved and always will solve the problems of the human race.

—Calvin Coolidge

I have not lost my desire to hear "fluffy" words, but I have gained a new appreciation for *my* word—PERSISTENT.

ANSWERED PRAYER

I was going through a spiritual down period for a week or so in 1985 and decided not to go to my prayer group meeting one night. My husband insisted that I go. I was very shy and rarely offered anything to the group, and I was not in the mood to hear about their answered prayers and praises.

Even though they never asked me to speak before, when I entered the meeting that night, they asked me if I had something I felt the need to share. Forgetting my shyness, I said, "Yes, but you won't like what I have to say." I explained that I had prayed so hard and my prayers were not answered.

Stacy Awalt, a former dance student of mine, had been diagnosed with leukemia when she was about seven years old. She had just died at age seventeen. I had prayed for her every day for ten years! The group asked me what would make me feel better about this. I explained that if I could only talk with her mother and see how she was doing, it might help. The problem was that I had lost contact with her over the years and saw no possibility of finding her. I did not know where she now lived or where she worked. My prayer group decided to pray for me during that week, and I was to return the next week to let them know how I felt.

During the ensuing week, I had to make phone calls to the area schools in order to schedule our Christmas performances with the various principals. When I called one of the schools, which I had called each year, the principal was out for the day. The school secretary asked if I would like to speak to the assistant principal, *Kay Awalt*—Stacy's mother. Needless to say, I went back to the prayer group to share our answered prayer!

LOVE WITH NO BARRIERS

I was a teenager in the 1950s and my father (I know now) was an alcoholic. Back then, I thought that he drank too much just because he wanted to, not knowing this condition was a disease that required treatment. I so much wanted a great relationship with my father, but my resentment for what I thought he was putting me through held me back.

I began praying every day. The words I used as a young girl were, "Lord, please wash away my resentment." These words became so much a part of me that I continued this same prayer daily, even as an adult. I loved my father through the years, but I knew there was a barrier that I, so much, wanted to break through.

When I was forty years old, I was sitting in a room filled with people at my sister's home. My dad was sitting on the sofa. I looked over at him and something that seemed like windshield wipers went back and forth across my eyes! I thought it was my contact lenses, so I adjusted them and it seemed to work *until* I looked at my father again. The windshield wipers came back. This continued a few more times—stopping when I looked away and starting again when I looked at my father.

Soon I thought of my daily prayer, and I felt water rushing gently through my mind and heart. When I again looked at my father, there was absolute love with no barriers.

The Lord did exactly what I had asked him to do—he *washed* away my resentment!

MY MENTAL JOURNEY

My husband was diagnosed with cancer, and one week later, he was to have a bone scan. If the cancer had not gone to his bones, it would be an indication that it was contained and a complete remission could be expected.

Each night, as I lay in bed beside him, I would mentally begin at his toes and pray *through* every bone in his body. Being a dance teacher certainly helped, because I have studied every bone! This process took practically an hour each night, but it always seemed like only minutes.

He had the bone scan and the doctor's statement, as he read the report, was, "We've rarely seen a bone scan so clear in a man your age!"

SEND ME AN ANGEL

Cancer is extremely frightening to me. After my husband had been diagnosed with cancer, I prayed constantly for him. One day I found myself praying for an angel to help us both.

I was at my dance studio and my daughter, who teaches for me, was coming in for her class. She was to go to the doctor that day to see if the thyroid problems she had been experiencing were cleared up. If she got a clean bill of health, she and her husband could begin trying to have the baby that they both wanted.

When I saw her coming in, I immediately asked her about the doctor's report. She ignored my question, and in a rush, began to tell me about a dream she had experienced the night before. She explained that she never dreamed, or if she did, she never remembered them. "This dream was so real!" she began to tell me. "A lady came into the studio and I was alone. Mom, I'm always afraid when I am by myself, but this lady was so warm and I immediately had no fear." She asked to see you and I explained to her that you had already gone home. She asked me to give you a message. The lady said, 'Would you tell your mom to stop worrying about your dad because he is healed?' Mom, she then hugged me and was gone." As tears began to fill my eyes, all I could say to her was, "Julie, God sent you the angel that I prayed for."

WORK IT OUT

When my husband Ray was in college we had two young sons. Paying bills was a real challenge. At the end of each month I would thank the Lord for seeing to it that we were able to *keep up* with our financial commitments.

Once we received an unexpected bill for $64.28 (a lot of money at that time). Ray was very concerned about our ability to pay this bill. I decided to ask the Lord to work this out. A few days later, a check came in the mail from the musicians' union for an engagement Ray had performed sometime earlier—for $64.28!

When we moved to Franklin in 1970, Ray had just received his doctorate; we had two young sons and an infant daughter; wonderful jobs at Peabody College and Vanderbilt University, and a home obtained with Ray's G.I. loan waiting for us. But, obviously, we were still strapped for money. We arrived with a U-Haul truck, our children, our car, and twenty dollars. When we got to our new home, the family who had sold it to us were still there! Someone had made a mistake! Our real estate agent said they would be gone in a week and that we could stay at the local Holiday Inn. We had a nice salary coming within a month but not enough for right now. On faith, we checked into the hotel and started our boys in elementary school. We ate by charging meals to our room with *no idea* how we would pay the bill, but we knew that the Lord wanted us to be here. At check-out time, the realtors met us at the front desk and said, "Our company is paying for the hotel stay and your meals since we got you here too early." Everything seems to work out when you do what *he* wants.

MAKE ME AWARE

When I am driving a car, I sometimes get caught up in what I am thinking or hearing on the radio, and my foot gets a little heavy on the gas pedal. Due to this little short-coming, I earned a couple of speeding tickets which I never told my husband about. You know, it is the whole mental process of not telling a loved one something that would just worry them—sort of like I do, sometimes, when I buy new clothes! Then, my husband was doing some type of insur-ance business with our agent and these speeding tickets *reared their ugly heads*. I was truly sorry to cause him this embarrassment, so I prayed for the Lord to make me aware of speed limits *from then on*.

Every time I get in my car now, I am *constantly* aware of speed limits. The Lord makes a wonderful co-pilot when you want him there.

PRAYERFUL
PATIENCE

My best friend and her husband divorced after some problems. I had taught their three daughters and saw the change of lifestyle and pain that they were suffering.

I began praying everyday that she and her ex-husband would eventually remarry. Over the years, they remained good friends. Each time I was with her, I would ask if she thought they would ever get back together and her answer was always no. I continued to pray.

After not seeing her for awhile, I recently felt a tremendous urge to ask her about the possibility of an upcoming marriage. She came to our home, and, after some casual conversation, I posed my question and she again said no. This made me wonder why it had seemed so important for me to talk to her.

Then, the very next day, she called to tell me that she had received a proposal *that day* and would be remarried to her former husband after thirteen years. Lord, our prayerful patience is always honored!

JUST ONE OF
THOUSANDS

David and Marian Smith from Natchez, Mississippi, came to visit us here in Franklin. Their son Michael came to our home with them. Michael had recently moved to Nashville as a bank examiner. I asked him if he had gotten to know anyone and he said that he had not but would love to meet someone just to spend time with. Immediately when he said that, Julie Johnson, a former student of mine, popped into my head.

I had not seen Julie for a long time and did not even know if she had a boyfriend or exactly what she was doing. Anyway, out of all the thousands of students that I have taught, why would *one particular* student come to mind so quickly? I know that answer—so I told him about her. I do not make it a habit to be a matchmaker, however.

I called Julie to see if it was all right to give him her phone number. It seems that she was now a nurse at a hospital in Nashville and was not seeing anyone seriously.

About four or five months later, I received some flowers and a card. The card read:

> You and the Lord were responsible for our meeting and we thank both of you. We are engaged to be married and our wedding will be in November.

AN ANGEL IN DISGUISE

Having never been on an airplane, I felt afraid as I prepared to take our baby son for a month-long visit with my husband's parents. My husband was going to Europe on a college-sponsored trip. I had a total of five dollars for the trip.

Flying alone and changing planes with a baby was almost too much for me. Before we boarded the first plane I prayed, "Lord, help us arrive safely, and help me find my way in the airports." I was afraid of getting on the wrong plane, so I prayed that I would arrive at my intended destination. I also prayed, "Let my guardian angel be by my side."

The first part of the trip my son slept as I looked out the window wondering what in the world kept airplanes in the air. We arrived at the airport and had about an hour layover to change planes. This would give me a chance to find my gate, feed my son, and get my boarding pass. Unfortunately, I took a wrong turn somewhere. By the time I found my gate, the plane was already boarding with a long line waiting outside in the rain and cold. My baby was hungry and crying; I was exhausted from carrying so much baby gear, a baby, and the carry-on luggage. Just before boarding, I was told that this plane was full and that I would have to wait for another plane—the next morning! I was frantic! Where would we stay? I only had the five dollars and not enough baby formula. The plane began to move out, heading for the runway, as I stood there crying desperately.

Suddenly I looked up and the airplane had stopped. The doors were opening, the stairs were rolled back to the door, and a man got off. He walked over to where I was standing behind a post and told me that he wanted me to take his seat. God had sent an angel to save me a seat.

OK—NO SHOES

Gene, the husband of my friend Jane, always teased Jane and me for our passion for shoes. When he was diagnosed with lung cancer, I would call him to see how he felt and tell him that I was praying for him. In spite of his condition, he continued to be a cutup, reminding me about my needless "hobby."

Eventually, Gene lapsed into a coma and was in the hospital. Jane stayed with him constantly. One day, when I went by to see them, she needed to go home and do some errands. I offered to stay with Gene. Knowing that people in a coma can still hear, I held an ongoing conversation with him while I tried to make him comfortable. When in a coma, patients often breath through their mouths, causing the mouth to be dry. I began putting moisture on his lips with a small swab. As I worked, I said to him, "Gene, after the angels come for you to take you to heaven, Jane and I will get together and have lunch and go shopping. We will probably even buy some shoes." Suddenly, he bit down on the stick as tightly as he could. I whispered, "Oh Gene, please let go. I'm afraid the swab will come off and you'll choke." He still held on. "Please let go." No luck! Then I realized what my last statement had been and I said, "OK, Gene, we won't buy shoes. We'll just go to lunch." Immediately, he opened his mouth and I began to laugh at his witty stunt.

Lord, thank you for letting our personality show through, even in a coma.

A JOB MADE
IN HEAVEN

A friend of mine was looking for a student to work after school in her dancewear shop. She asked me if I knew of anyone. I told her I did not but that I would pray about it so we could find the right person. I love to find my students good after-school jobs where the employer understands their time commitment to their dance education.

While shopping one Sunday afternoon, I saw a student and her mother. While I was talking to her, that job kept popping into my head. At the end of our conversation I said, "I realize that you have never told me that you needed, or even wanted, a job after school, but I feel I must be obedient and ask you if that is a possibility." She looked completely shocked. She had just been talking to her mother about going to the dancewear shop to apply for a job. It seems her dad had lost his job and she wanted to help out.

TICKETS TO GO

Jan has been a dear friend to me for many years. We never really got to visit much since she was busy with her piano students and I with my dance students. In order to see her more, I decided to take piano lessons from her.

At one of my lessons, Jan mentioned a choir concert that she and her husband wanted us to attend. Because my husband was working so much, I didn't want to ask him to go someplace unless I knew he truly wanted to go. The concert was on a Sunday night, which was his only night off.

To Jan and me, this sounded like something for the Lord to handle. We both prayed, "Lord, give him the desire to go to this concert." The next night my husband came home with tickets for *this very concert*!

SPIRITUAL
FRIENDS

As my friend Betty's cancer progressed, I strongly felt that she needed someone to meet her spiritual needs. Her minister and the members of her church were wonderful, but I felt that she wanted something more. While praying for that need, I suddenly thought of my friends Vaughn and Brenda. Because I knew that they were extremely busy, I almost did not call them. Knowing that I would get no peace until I was obedient, I called.

The Holy Spirit makes it impossible to get my mind on other things unless I do what is asked of me. Vaughn told me that he and his wife had been working with many cancer patients and would be honored to meet with Betty.

It was a match made in heaven! They became wonderful friends and saw her daily until she died. Each day, Betty wore the praying hands necklace that Vaughn and Brenda had given her. On the day that she passed away, her daughters gave the necklace to their grandmother. I can't imagine the void in Betty's life without this gift from Vaughn and Brenda. Thank you, Lord, for forcing me to listen.

PERFECT TIMING

Traveling is not one of my favorite things to do. I love being in new and different places but I do not like getting to and from the cities in airplanes, cars, trains, ships, or buses. They all frighten me. It seems ridiculous to me for so many people to put their lives in the hands of one imperfect human being. What if that person had a fuss with a family member or had some tragedy occur in his/her life? He/she may not be concentrating like one should. I still travel in these modes of transportation, but the airplane scares me the most, especially in icy weather.

My husband and I were going to Oklahoma City for a meeting with one of the deans of Oklahoma University. The weather channel was predicting very cold, icy weather at the time of our departure and also at the time of our arrival home. When I got scared, I started finding reasons that I should not go, even after the tickets had been purchased. My husband did not appreciate this and wished that I would have told him I did not want to go before he purchased the tickets. Since I knew that no matter what, I was going to be sitting on the airplane at 6:30 A.M. with ice and freezing rain, I started my prayers.

The bad weather was predicted to arrive in our area by morning and again the next day at the time of our return flight from Oklahoma. As we left for the airport, the storm had not arrived yet. It was still warm! When we returned, the weather had come and gone. Lord, your timing was perfect—just like our airplane ride.

ONE CALL

It was spring break and many of my students headed to Florida—each to a different part of the Sunshine State. My husband and I had decided to relax at home for the week and not travel. I was leaving home on a shopping trip when the phone rang. I do not even remember who it was that called, but the message was devastating. Melanie and Kacy, best friends who were both students of mine, were in Florida somewhere with their families.

There had been a terrible swimming accident due to a strong undertow. Melanie's mother was in a hospital in critical condition. Melanie's father and Kacy's mother had drowned, in knee-deep water. I was so much in shock that I failed to ask the person who called what city and hospital they were in or the conditions of any other family members. Knowing how close Melanie and I had always been, I knew that I should try to comfort her immediately.

I prayed for the Lord to help me find her as soon as possible. I randomly telephoned one hospital in Florida and asked for Melanie. She came to the phone!

I PROMISE

"When you make a promise, it is a vow not to be broken." My mother told me this on our screened-in porch when I was in the third grade. She said, "don't make a promise unless you plan to keep it!" It made *such* an impression on me.

In the fifth grade, the girl sitting in front of me turned around and told me that she had an accident in her pants. With tears rolling down her face she said, "promise me that you won't tell anyone." I felt so sorry for her and I promised her that I would tell no one. Well, the urine ran *under my desk* instead of hers! Everyone thought that I did it. They teased me the rest of the day as the girl to whom I had made the promise watched from a distance. I did not understand how she could see me crying and so hurt and not tell the truth. Why, Lord? All I could think of, though, was to keep my promise.

Thirty-five years later I saw her when I was visiting my hometown of Natchez, Mississippi. After a long conversation about what has happened in our lives, she apologized to me for that incident. She also told me that I had made such an impression on her that day that she had spent the last thirty-five years trying to be *just like me*. What an honor I had achieved!

You never know when a day or so of your pain may change someone's life. What a joy it is to live long enough to see the "whys" for some of our questions.

Thank you, Lord!

LET US BE CONNECTED

Megan's father had been sick for a long time but he was getting worse. I had told Megan, an eight-year-old student, that if she ever needed to talk, I was always willing to listen. One afternoon the phone rang and it was Megan. She said that her dad was in a coma now and she was so frightened. "I want to stay close to him," she told me. We talked awhile until she asked me if I could come over to her home immediately. Without hesitation, I said that I would be right there. I got the directions to her home, which seemed very complicated since I have little sense of direction, and it was south of Franklin in a place I had never been. Also, my eyesight is not the best, especially in unfamiliar places.

I prayed that my presence with her would give her comfort and that I could say or do something that would help her through this difficult time. I also prayed that I could *find* her! As I hurriedly started to leave my home, I opened a little ceramic box and found two gold angels— one small and one large. During the trip, I decided that the larger angel could be for her dad to wear and the smaller one would be for Megan. My next thought was one that kept pounding in my head, "It has to be Megan's idea." The Holy Spirit has to work overtime with me and I appreciate the persistence because I *want* to do the Lord's will at all times.

I kept driving, thinking, and praying until I drove into her driveway! That doesn't sound like much of a feat but finding my way is not one of my best abilities—it was definitely divine intervention. When I arrived at her home, Megan and her mom were standing outside waiting for me. Her mom left Megan and me alone. We sat down and I held her as she told me how much she was going to miss her dad. As she cried in my arms, the Lord put in my mind the way to give Megan the gold angels.

I asked her if she had ever seen the necklaces that friends wear—one necklace having half of a heart and the other having the other half. Megan said that she had seen them and that they were worn so that friends could feel connected to each other. After she told me that, I gave her the angels. She thanked me and said, "Mrs. Ann, I can pin the large one on my dad and I can wear the little one—then we can always be connected!"

Megan was so excited, she asked me to go in with her to pin the angel on her dad. Having been told that people in a coma can hear, she jumped up on his bed and said, "Dad, do you remember Mrs. Ann? She has given us some angels to wear to keep us connected."

As she pinned the angel on him, she explained to him that he would wear his in heaven and she would wear hers here everyday. When her dad passed away, she pinned the angel on his suit at the funeral. I have seen her angel pinned on her leotard as she danced in class.

Lord, you work in the sweetest ways—a little angel wears a little angel.

A NEED FOR APPLAUSE

Everyone needs applause. Everyone *deserves* applause. Everyone will see to it that they get applause in some way at sometime. The dictionary explains that applause is

approval expressed by clapping the hands or shouting; praise.

People in the performance field are very fortunate because they hear a roar of clapping hands after a job well-done or for their effort. I wish everyone in all fields could experience that sound.

We are all seeking approval and praise. It comes to us in a smile, a handshake, a hug, a kind word, a card, a flower, a nod. We do not need a stage, curtain, music, or lights.

A wife or husband preparing a special meal is cause for applause.

A special report at work; doing a minor task for someone who needs it is cause for applause.

Anything that is a little out of the ordinary or unexpected is cause for applause.

Failing to achieve approval and praise is like a beautiful plant trying to survive without water. Since we will always *strive* for applause, if it is not given to us when we feel we deserve it, we *will* get attention in other ways not so pleasing. I know we have all watched people in meetings who keep the attention of everyone by disagreeing on all or most subjects when it really makes no difference—that person is starved for applause. The child who would rather have negative attention than no attention is also starved for applause.

A wife or husband may eventually quit trying to please the other because the efforts go unnoticed. If we keep our eyes and ears open, ready to show a random act of kindness, eventually we will get our needed approval or praise.

Do you think that the Lord sometimes feels that he needs a bit more approval or praise for the many things that he does for us that go unnoticed? We must stop, look, and listen to become constantly aware of his attention to us. I would say that his works for us are a definite cause for applause.

Lord, please help us praise you for all things and let us be more aware of others who need our applause.

CHEER US TO HEAVEN

Cheerleader tryouts always end up being a happy time for some of my students and a sad time for others. Some of my students are able to shake off the pain of losing by saying, "At least I have my dance to throw myself into." Each year I try to comfort them in class.

I recently had a tremendous urge to call one of my students who had just moved to Franklin this school year and ask her to demonstrate for me next year. She was asleep when I called, but her mom and I talked for a long time. It seems that one of her daughters had made cheerleader and one had not. The mother was in so much pain, the kind that all parents feel when they see their children hurting. Her husband was out of town and she needed someone to talk to. The daughter who had not been chosen as a cheerleader was the one that I called to become a demonstrator because of her sweet, gentle spirit. The young students love this type of role model.

I asked her about demonstrating the next day during class, and I immediately saw a happy, self-confident, beautiful person emerge from one who had cried all night over her feelings of rejection.

Lord, I wish that our precious children could be spared from that pain. Our pain, for our children, must be how *you* feel for us when we are hurting. Many young girls want to be cheerleaders, and it hurts when they do not achieve their goal. I know there are good reasons why some do not make it. Lord, please lead them in the direction that you want them to take.

PART THREE

THE CIRCLE'S COMPLETE

FOR MY STUDENTS

I wish for them to make the Lord the center of their lives. To go to church and Sunday School regularly—not only to get a special blessing from it, but to give time back to the Lord. To learn from all of their mistakes. To learn from older people. To make wise decisions. To think about consequences resulting from their actions. To have the desire to do the right things. To show no jealousy towards others. To feel good about themselves without hurting others. To learn to pray constantly and persistently. To obey their parents. To know that it is more difficult for a parent to say no than to give in to their every wish. To do their best in school and learn as much as they can. To be responsible. To be trusted. To be honorable. To be happy. To realize that God does not make junk. To keep their bodies in good working order. To put into their bodies only good things. To be thankful for little things. To learn to laugh at themselves. To be helpful to others. To understand that parents were given no instructions on how to raise children—they do the best they can. To learn to appreciate small things. To do something good for someone each day. To be the best *you* possible. To get excited about going to school. To let little things excite them. To know that discipline is a form of love. To say "thank you" often. To thank their parents for loving each other so much that they gave birth to them. To be interested—not interesting. To be pleasing—not expecting to be pleased. To be lovable—not waiting to be loved. To avoid anything in their lives that would be unworthy of the gospel of Christ. To be considerate. To be better than average—being average is unworthy of their possibilities. To always be willing to forgive—forgiving is a decision. To be a good family member. To be able to forgive themselves. To be aware of great opportunities brilliantly disguised as impossible situations. To be patient. To be optimistic. To have great attitudes. To be happy and healthy—it begins in the head. To understand that religion is love. To know that they cannot depend on others for their happiness. To love their neighbors as themselves. To know that the better they feel about themselves, the more they can love someone else. To be able to accept a compliment—it is the lifeblood and the heartbeat of a relationship. To always wake up saying, "Good morning, God!" not "Good God, morning!" To love persons—not things. To praise God for every situation. To thank God for who they are.

BECAUSE OF YOU

I wish you could *know* what you mean to me.
I wish you could *feel* how sharing your life can be.
I wish you could *see* that masterpiece I see.
Because of you—I've seen miracles.

Thank you, Lord, so graciously.
Thank you for the success you've made me know.
Thank you for your love that has warmed me so.
Thank you for sharing your life while you grow,
Because of you—I've seen miracles.

Thank you, Lord, I love you—you know.
Sharing your thoughts with all that you hope and dream,
Sharing your laughter, those sounds make me beam.
Sharing your life makes me feel like a queen.
Because of you—I've seen miracles.

Thank you, Lord, I've seen.

FOR ALL TEACHERS

I wish for all teachers to realize that they have a tremendous impact on their students' lives. To build their self-confidence. To make learning fun. To watch for loners. To go to church—let them see you there. To let God be the center of their lives. To be a good example. To praise their students for small things. To be aware of problems. To be interested in each child. To never allow their personal problems to affect class. To be happy. To show respect for the students. To listen to them. To love them. To make an impression on them. To be remembered as their favorite teacher—the one who expected the most, taught them the most, and loved them the most.

FOR ALL
PARENTS

I wish for all parents to enjoy every minute of their children's lives. To keep their spouse number one. To be tough but tender. To be interested in their children's activities. To pray a lot. To take their children to church and Sunday School. To participate in their activities. To feed them healthy food. To discipline with love. To be consistent. To agree on decisions about their children. To not let their children play one against the other. To watch them carefully in the early teen years. To set rules and keep them. To do what they say they are going to do. To tell them they are loved daily. To expect a lot from them with some leeway to falter. To praise their children for small achievements—this is easy in the early years and more difficult as they get older. To not put too much pressure on them to win—there is a fine line between showing interest and showing that you desperately want them to win. To not worry about their children's popularity—some of the most unpopular people have become the most successful. To remember that the most important thing is that their children become wonderful adults. To teach them responsibility. To teach them honesty. To teach them to love by loving them. To keep them busy enough to stay out of trouble. To show respect for their children. To build beautiful memories. To set family traditions. To teach them to control their temper. To know that children learn by their example.

FOR MY CHILDREN

Mom is a special title that is earned in many ways. It is the most important title a woman can achieve. Everytime I hear you call me *Mom* it feels like a wonderful compliment that I am striving to reach but have not quite deserved yet. To be such a small word, it has so much meaning.

When you call me *Mom*, it reminds me of my parents who worked so hard to do their very best for me. They made me what I am today.

When you call me *Mom*, it reminds me of the love and devotion that your dad and I share, even though the struggles of everyday life try to break down a marriage.

When you call me *Mom*, it reminds me of the birth of each one of you—the miracles you are and the joy you have brought to us.

When you call me *Mom*, it reminds me of the sleepless nights, the illnesses that scared me, the trials of being consistent, and all the times that I did not feel like I measured up to the title, but you felt I did.

When you call me *Mom*, it reminds me of the mates that you have chosen and how easy it is to love them because they love you.

When you call me *Mom,* it reminds me of your children—our grandchildren—who have certainly added excitement and fun to all of our days. What a joy it is to hear them call *you* Mom and Dad.

When you call me *Mom,* it reminds me of the fun times we have when we are all together talking and sharing our daily trials and triumphs. I feel so proud when I see all of you in one place, laughing and loving each other.

When you call me *Mom,* it reminds me of the contentment I have in watching you become such happy, loving, caring, sharing, spiritual people, striving to be the best *you* possible.

When I feel, sometimes, that I am not worthy of that title and that I am your *Model of Mediocrity*—all I need is to hear you call me *Mom,* and you make me feel like a *Master of Motherhood.* Thanks for the honor you have given to me.

I love you all,
Your Mom

FULL CIRCLE DANCE

Dance, children, dance.
So happy you'll be.
Please dance for the Lord.
That's a wish from me.

Dance through your worries.
Dance through your pain.
Dance through your prayers.
The Lord knows your name.

Dance over dangers.
Dance over falls.
Dance over troubles,
'Til the Lord makes his call.

Dance when you're happy.
Dance when you're sad.
Dance when your life
Goes from good to bad.
Dance when you're young,
So innocent and sweet.
Dance when you're keeping
All the friends that you meet.

Dance when you're a teen
And your life's in a maze.
Dance as you count
Each one of the days.

Dance when you leave
For your college adventure.
Dance when you meet
The man of your future.

Dance as you become
What you worked hard to be.
Dance when your goals
Have been reached and you see.

Dance as you marry
The man of your dreams.
Dance as his love
Makes you feel like a queen.
Dance as your child
Is born—it's a girl.
Dance as she grows
And takes you for a whirl.

Dance as *her* dancing
Sweeps you off your feet.
She's dancing with me.
The circle's complete.

ABOUT THE AUTHOR

ANN CARROLL has directed her School of Dance in Franklin, Tennessee, for thirty-six years, growing the school to be one of the largest and most successful in the South. Carroll has served as president of the Southern Association of Dance Masters, an organization representing dance teachers in fourteen states, and is an active member of the Dance Educators of America.

Known lovingly by her pupils as "Mrs. Ann," former students of Carroll's can be found appearing in Broadway productions, motion pictures, professional dance companies, and on television. A select group of her dancers have performed at the White House. Also, fittingly, many students have followed in Carroll's footsteps and are dance teachers themselves.

Ann Carroll lives in Franklin, Tennessee, with her husband Ray. They have four children and are the proud grandparents of four (soon to be six).